~A BINGO BOOK~

Montana Bingo Book

COMPLETE BINGO GAME IN A BOOK

MONTANA

ORO -Y- PLATA

Written By Rebecca Stark
Educational Books 'n' Bingo

Educational Books 'n' Bingo

ISBN 978-0-87386-519-7

Printed in the U.S.A.

DIRECTIONS

INCLUDED:

List of Terms

Templates for Additional Terms and Clues

2 Clues per Term

30 Unique Bingo Cards

Markers

1. **Either cut apart the book or make copies of ALL the sheets. You might want to make an extra copy of the clue sheets to use for introduction and review. Keep the sheets in an envelope for easy reuse.**

2. Cut apart the call cards with terms and clues.

3. Pass out one bingo card per student. There are enough for a class of 30.

4. Pass out markers. You may cut apart the markers included in this book or use any other small items of your choice.

5. Decide whether or not you will require the entire card to be filled. Requiring the entire card to be filled provides a better review. However, if you have a short time to fill, you may prefer to have them do the just the border or some other format. Tell the class before you begin what is required.

6. There are 50 terms. Read the list before you begin. If there are any terms that have not been covered in class, you may want to read to the students the term and clues before you begin.

7. There is a blank space in the middle of each card. You can instruct the students to use it as a free space or you can write in answers to cover terms not included. Of course, in this case you would create your own clues. (Templates provided.)

8. Shuffle the cards and place them in a pile. Two or three clues are provided for each term. If you plan to play the game with the same group more than once, you might want to choose a different clue for each game. If not, you may choose to use more than one clue.

9. Be sure to keep the cards you have used for the present game in a separate pile. When a student calls, "Bingo," he or she will have to verify that the correct answers are on his or her card AND that the markers were placed in response to the proper questions. Pull out the cards that are on the student's card keeping them in the order they were used in the game. Read each clue as it was given and ask the student to identify the correct answer from his or her card.

10. If the student has the correct answers on the card AND has shown that they were marked in response to the *correct questions,* then that student is the winner and the game is over. If the student does not have the correct answers on the card OR he or she marked the answers in response to *the wrong questions,* then the game continues until there is a proper winner.

11. If you want to play again, reshuffle the cards and begin again.

Have fun!

TERMS INCLUDED

Billings

Bison

Bitterroot

Blackspotted Cutthroat Trout

Bluebunch Wheatgrass

Borders (-ed)

Butte

Cattle

Climate

Continental Divide

Copper

County (-ies)

Crop(s)

Executive Branch

Flag

Flathead

Fort Benton

Fort Peck Dam

Gemstone(s)

Glacier National Park

Gold

Granite Peak

Great Falls

Great Plains

Grizzly Bear(s)

Helena

Industry (-ies)

Judicial

Legislature

Lewis and Clark

Louisiana Purchase

Maiasaura

Makoshika State Park

Missoula

Missouri River

Motto

Nickname

Oregon Treaty

Ponderosa Pine

Reservation(s)

River(s)

Rocky Mountains

Sacajawea

Seal

Sioux

Songs

Territory (-ies)

Union

Western Meadowlark(s)

Yellowstone National Park

Montana Bingo

Additional Terms

Choose as many additional terms as you would like and write them in the squares. Repeat each as desired.
Cut out the squares and randomly distribute them to the class.
Instruct the students to place their square on the center space of their card.

Montana Bingo

© Barbara M. Peller

Clues for Additional Terms

Write three clues for each of your additional terms.

_____ 1. 2. 3.	_____ 1. 2. 3.
_____ 1. 2. 3.	_____ 1. 2. 3.
_____ 1. 2. 3.	_____ 1. 2. 3.

Montana Bingo

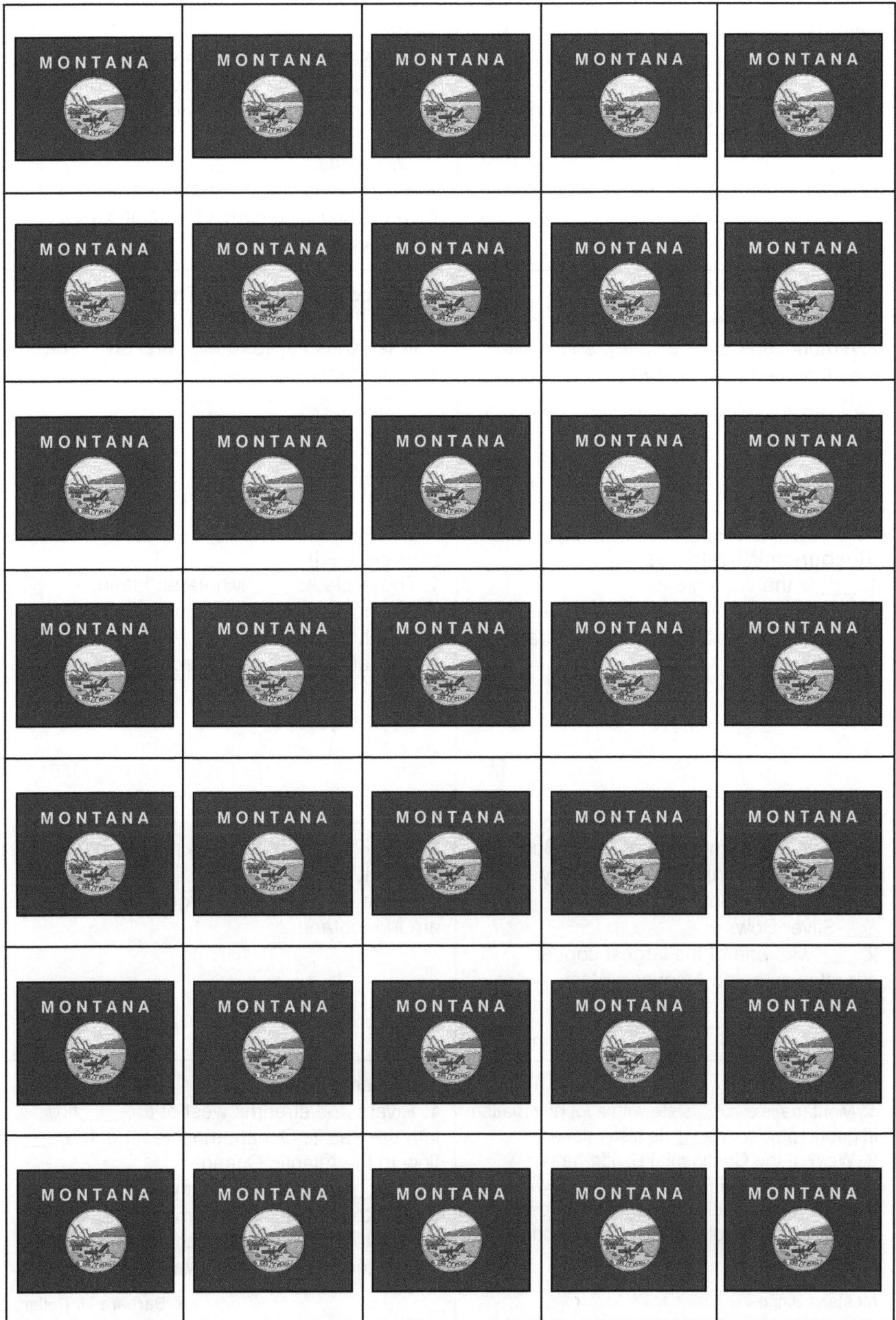

Billings 1. ___ is the largest city in Montana. 2. ___ was a rail hub founded by the Northern Pacific Railroad. It was named for a former president of that railroad.	**Bison** 1. The National ___ Range was established in 1908 and is one of the oldest wildlife refuges in the nation. Its entrance is in Moiese. From 350 to 500 ___ roam the 18,500-acres. 2. A ___ skull is on the state quarter. It is a sacred symbol to many of Montana's American Indian tribes.
Bitterroot 1. ___ is the state flower. 2. A mountain range, a valley, and a river are all named for this flower.	**Blackspotted Cutthroat Trout** 1. The ___ is the state fish. 2. This fish is native to Montana and is on the threatened-species list.
Bluebunch Wheatgrass 1. ___ is the state grass. 2. ___ grows in most soil. It protrudes above the early snows, providing forage for livestock.	**Borders (-ed)** 1. These states ___ Montana: Idaho, Wyoming, North Dakota, South Dakota, and Idaho. 2. Montana is ___ by Canada on the north.
Butte 1. ___ is the county seat of Silver Bow County. In 1977, the city and county governments consolidated to form ___-Silver Bow. 2. ___ was one of the largest copper boomtowns in the American West.	**Cattle** 1. Beef ___ are Montana's most important livestock product. 2. Some of the nation's largest ___ ranches are in Montana.
Climate 1. Montana is a large state with a lot of variation in geography, so the ___ is also varied. 2. West of the Continental Divide has a modified Northern Pacific Coast ___, with milder winters, cooler summers, and less wind. East of the divide has a semi-arid, continental ___. Montana Bingo	**Continental Divide** 1. Rivers and streams west of the ___ flow into the Pacific Ocean; those east of the ___ flow to the Atlantic Ocean. 2. The ___ separates the river systems that drain into the Pacific Ocean from those that drain into the Atlantic Ocean. It crosses into the United States in northwestern Montana. © **Barbara M. Peller**

Copper

1. Industrialists William Andrews Clark, Marcus Daly, and F. Augustus Heinze fought over control of the ___-mining industry in and around Butte.
2. Daly's Anaconda ___ Mining Company emerged as a monopoly. From 1892 through 1903, the Anaconda mine was the largest ___-producing mine in the world.

County (-ies)

1. Montana is divided into 56 ___.
2. Yellowstone is the largest ___ in population. The largest ___ by area is Beaverhead.

Crop(s)

1. Wheat, barley, hay, beans, potatoes, sugar beets and black cherries are important ___.
2. Wheat is the most important ___.

Executive Branch

1. The ___ of state government comprises the governor, the lieutenant governor, the secretary of state, the state auditor, the attorney general, and the superintendent of public instruction.
2. The governor is the top official in the ___ of state government. The present-day governor is [fill in].

Flag

1. The Montana ___ displays the state seal on a field of deep blue.
2. The word "MONTANA" appears in gold letters above the seal on the state ___.

Flathead

1. ___ Lake is the largest natural freshwater lake in the state. Once known as "Salish Lake," it takes its name from the Native Americans who live in the reservation at its southern end.
2. The ___ National Forest is in the Rocky Mountains, west of the Continental Divide and just south of the Canadian border.

Fort Benton

1. ___ was founded as the last fur trading post on the Upper Missouri River. It became an important economic center.
2. Founded in 1847, ___ is called the "Birthplace of Montana." It is now a National Historic Landmark.

Fort Peck Dam

1. ___ is the highest of six major dams along the Missouri River and the largest hydraulically filled dam in the United States.
2. ___ was created a lake by the same name. It is the fifth largest man-made lake in the United States.

Gemstone(s)

1. Montana has two official ___: Montana agate and the sapphire.
2. The sapphire is one of Montana's two state ___. Montana sapphires have remarkable color and brilliance. There are some colors that are found no where else in the world.

Glacier National Park

1. In 1910 ___ became the country's 10th national park. It is known for its rugged peaks, clear waters, and glacial-carved valleys. Several National Historic Landmarks are within the park.
2. Grinnell Glacier is in ___. It is named for a conservationist and explorer who advocated the park's creation.

Montana Bingo

Gold 1. In 1862, prospectors found ___ in Grasshopper Creek, which is in the area now part of southwestern Montana, then part of Idaho territory. 2. Virginia City and Nevada City lie along Alder Gulch, the site of the richest ___ strike in the Rocky Mountains in the 1860s.	**Granite Peak** 1. At 12,799 feet, ___ is the highest point in the state. 2. ___, the highest point in Montana, lies within the Absaroka-Beartooth Wilderness, 10 miles north of the Wyoming border.
Great Falls 1. ___ is the third largest city in Montana. 2. This city takes its name from the series of five waterfalls in close proximity along the upper Missouri River Basin.	**Great Plains** 1. The ___ Region is made up of high, gently rolling land interrupted by hills and wide river valleys, including the Yellowstone and Missouri rivers. 2. The eastern 3/5 of Montana is covered by the ___. The Rocky Mountains cover the western 2/5 of the state.
Grizzly Bear(s) 1. The ___ is the state animal. ___ are the largest carnivores of North America. 2. These powerful animals can be found in Glacier National Park and the mountains of northwest Montana.	**Helena** 1. ___ is the state capital. 2. ___ was founded with the 1864 discovery of gold in a gulch off the Prickly Pear Valley. The city's main street is named Last Chance Gulch.
Industry (-ies) 1. Montana's major ___ involve the processing of raw materials from mines, forests, and farms. 2. The refining of petroleum refineries is a major ___ in Montana.	**Judicial** 1. The highest court in the state's ___ is the Supreme Court. It comprises a chief justice and 6 associate justices. Unlike most states, there is no intermediate appellate court; the Supreme Court hears all appeals. 2. The ___ interprets our laws. It is in charge of the court system.
Legislature 1. The Montana ___ comprises the Senate and the House of Representatives. 2. The ___ makes the laws.	**Lewis and Clark** 1. The ___ Expedition was also known as the Corps of Discovery. 2. The objective of the ___ Expedition was to study the lands acquired by the Louisiana Purchase and to find a practical water route across the continent.
Montana Bingo	

Louisiana Purchase 1. The United States acquired most of what is now Montana as part of the Louisiana Purchase of 1803. 2. The ___ doubled the size of the United States.	**Maiasaura** 1. The ___ *peeblesorum* is the state fossil. It was a hadrosaur, or duck-billed dinosaur. 2. ___ lived in the area that is now Montana during the Upper Cretaceous period. The area where the fossils were found is called Egg Mountain.
Makoshika State Park 1. ___ is the largest of Montana's state parks. Triceratops, Edmontosaurus, Tyrannosaurus, and other dinosaur fossils have been found here. 2. ___ features badlands formations and the fossil remains of a *Tyrannosaurus rex.* It is in eastern Montana east of Glendive.	**Missoula** 1. ___ is the second largest city in Montana. The Veterans' Memorial Rose Garden is in this city. 2. The main campus of the University of Montana is located in ___.
Missouri River 1. The ___ is the longest river in North America and a major waterway of the central United States. It is a tributary of the Mississippi River. 2. The ___ rises in the Rocky Mountains of western Montana.	**Motto** 1. The state ___ is "Oro y Plata"; it is on the Great Seal. 2. An English translation of the state ___ is "Gold and Silver."
Nickname 1. The official ___ for Montana is "The Treasure State" because of its rich mineral reserves. 2. The ___ "Big Sky Country" was made popular by a Montana State Highway Department promotion in the 1960s.	**Oregon Treaty** 1. As a result of the Oregon Treaty of 1846, Great Britain gave the remaining portion of Montana to the United States. 2. The ___ settled competing American and British claims to the Oregon Country, which had been occupied by both since the Treaty of 1818.
Ponderosa Pine 1. The ___ is the state tree. It can be found in most parts of western Montana. 2. Pioneers used ___ timber everywhere from railroad ties and telegraph poles to homes. Montana Bingo	**Reservation(s)** 1. The Crow Indian ___ in southern Montana is the largest one in the state. 2. Native American ___ in Montana include Blackfeet Nation, Chippewa Cree Tribe, Confederated Salish & Kootenai Tribes, Crow Tribal Council, Fort Belknap Indian Community, Fort Peck Indian Community, and Northern Cheyenne. © **Barbara M. Peller**

River(s) 1. The headwaters of the Missouri ___ rise in the Rocky Mountains of Montana. The Clark Fork and the Yellowstone are other important ___ in the state. 2. The Clark Fork is Montana's largest ___ by volume.	**Rocky Mountains** 1. The eastern 3/5 of Montana is covered by the Great Plains. The ___ cover the western 2/5 of the state. 2. There are more than 50 mountain ranges in the ___ Region of the state.
Sacajawea 1. This Shoshone Indian woman was born near the Continental Divide at the present-day Idaho-Montana border. 2. ___ accompanied the Lewis and Clark Expedition. She acted as interpreter and helped them obtain horses from the Shoshone.	**Seal** 1. The Great ___ displays symbols of Montana's natural beauty: a sunrise, waterfalls, mountains, hills, trees, and cliffs. 2. The Great ___ also displays symbols of the state's mining and farming history: a pick, a shovel, and a plow.
Sioux 1. The ___ were successful at the Battle of Little Big Horn River, also known as Custer's Last Stand. 2. Crazy Horse and Gall were two ___ leaders.	**Songs** 1. Montana has 3 official state ___: "Montana Melody," "Montana Lullaby," and "Montana." 2. "Montana" was adopted as the official state ___ in 1945. The first line is "Tell me of that Treasure State."
Territory (-ies) 1. At various times, parts of what is now Montana were parts of the ___ of Louisiana, Missouri, Nebraska, Dakota, Oregon, Washington, and Idaho. 2. On May 26, 1864, President Lincoln signed an act creating the Montana ___. Bannack was chosen as its first capital.	**Union** 1. Montana was admitted to the ___ as a state on November 8, 1889. 2. When Montana joined the ___ in 1889, it became the 41st state.
Western Meadowlark(s) 1. The ___ is the state bird. 2. Adult ___ have a black and white striped head; a long, pointed bill; yellow cheeks; a bright yellow throat; and a distinctive black "V" on the breast.	**Yellowstone National Park** 1. ___ is the world's first national park as well as one of the largest. Congress created it in 1872. 2. ___ is mostly in Wyoming, but it extends into Montana and Idaho.

Montana Bingo

Montana Bingo

Oregon Treaty	Billings	Bitterroot	Gemstone(s)	Bluebunch Wheatgrass
Fort Benton	Bison	Western Meadowlark(s)	Lewis and Clark	River(s)
Union	Legislature		Missouri River	Sacajawea
Territory (-ies)	Reservation(s)	Songs	Judicial	Maiasaura
Missoula	Granite Peak	Executive Branch	Seal	Grizzly Bear(s)

Montana Bingo

Territory (-ies)	Union	Great Plains	Ponderosa Pine	Industry (-ies)
Maiasaura	Flag	Cattle	Reservation(s)	Makoshika State Park
Continental Divide	Granite Peak		Great Falls	Songs
Motto	Nickname	Legislature	Yellowstone National Park	Bluebunch Wheatgrass
River(s)	Western Meadowlark(s)	Executive Branch	Fort Benton	Seal

Montana Bingo

Granite Peak	Songs	Flag	Judicial	Union
Maiasaura	Bison	Climate	Billings	Gold
Reservation(s)	Western Meadowlark(s)		Makoshika State Park	Blackspotted Cutthroat Trout
Legislature	Continental Divide	Missoula	Motto	Great Plains
Seal	Copper	Executive Branch	Yellowstone National Park	Industry (-ies)

Montana Bingo: Card No. 3

Montana Bingo

Legislature	Makoshika State Park	Bitterroot	Copper	Industry (-ies)
Louisiana Purchase	Butte	Billings	Ponderosa Pine	Union
Missouri River	Motto		Grizzly Bear(s)	Gemstone(s)
Songs	Bison	Western Meadowlark(s)	Executive Branch	Cattle
County (-ies)	River(s)	Borders (-ed)	Seal	Sacajawea

Montana Bingo

River(s)	Bluebunch Wheatgrass	Reservation(s)	Cattle	Copper
Louisiana Purchase	Songs	Climate	Great Falls	Bison
Bitterroot	Sacajawea		Lewis and Clark	Glacier National Park
Grizzly Bear(s)	Industry (-ies)	Oregon Treaty	Yellowstone National Park	Crop(s)
Flag	Executive Branch	Union	Legislature	Missouri River

Montana Bingo

Blackspotted Cutthroat Trout	Makoshika State Park	Great Plains	Industry (-ies)	Sacajawea
Judicial	Reservation(s)	Crop(s)	Billings	Union
Ponderosa Pine	County (-ies)		Butte	Great Falls
Executive Branch	Missoula	Yellowstone National Park	Borders (-ed)	Bitterroot
Maiasaura	Cattle	Oregon Treaty	Missouri River	Flathead

Montana Bingo

Oregon Treaty	Makoshika State Park	Glacier National Park	Songs	Flag
Maiasaura	Industry (-ies)	Granite Peak	Bison	Louisiana Purchase
Sacajawea	Gemstone(s)		Great Falls	Butte
Legislature	Motto	Climate	Territory (-ies)	Continental Divide
Executive Branch	Copper	Yellowstone National Park	Borders (-ed)	Blackspotted Cutthroat Trout

Montana Bingo

Missouri River	Makoshika State Park	Fort Peck Dam	Judicial	Butte
Louisiana Purchase	Bitterroot	Ponderosa Pine	Sacajawea	Cattle
Flathead	Copper		Industry (-ies)	Bluebunch Wheatgrass
Seal	Legislature	Territory (-ies)	County (-ies)	Motto
Western Meadowlark(s)	Executive Branch	Borders (-ed)	Reservation(s)	Maiasaura

Montana Bingo

Great Falls	Flag	Granite Peak	Flathead	Copper
County (-ies)	Industry (-ies)	Missouri River	Reservation(s)	Makoshika State Park
Gold	Oregon Treaty		Bison	Fort Peck Dam
Crop(s)	Bluebunch Wheatgrass	Missoula	Lewis and Clark	Glacier National Park
Motto	Yellowstone National Park	Climate	Territory (-ies)	Grizzly Bear(s)

Montana Bingo

Territory (-ies)	Judicial	Butte	Ponderosa Pine	Flathead
Sacajawea	Cattle	Billings	Bison	Industry (-ies)
Copper	Makoshika State Park		Gemstone(s)	Continental Divide
Missoula	Grizzly Bear(s)	Crop(s)	Yellowstone National Park	Gold
Climate	Maiasaura	Great Plains	River(s)	Missouri River

Montana Bingo: Card No. 10

Montana Bingo

Blackspotted Cutthroat Trout	Makoshika State Park	Reservation(s)	Crop(s)	Maiasaura
Fort Peck Dam	Gold	Lewis and Clark	Great Falls	Billings
Louisiana Purchase	Industry (-ies)		Great Plains	Granite Peak
Climate	Union	Yellowstone National Park	Copper	Territory (-ies)
County (-ies)	Executive Branch	Oregon Treaty	Borders (-ed)	Flag

© Barbara M. Peller

Montana Bingo

Flag	Bluebunch Wheatgrass	Gold	Judicial	Great Falls
Granite Peak	Maiasaura	Bitterroot	Borders (-ed)	Bison
Oregon Treaty	Glacier National Park		Sacajawea	Ponderosa Pine
Executive Branch	Motto	Industry (-ies)	Territory (-ies)	Louisiana Purchase
Makoshika State Park	Fort Peck Dam	Copper	County (-ies)	Cattle

Montana Bingo

Crop(s)	Bluebunch Wheatgrass	Blackspotted Cutthroat Trout	Gold	Sacajawea
Bitterroot	Fort Peck Dam	Industry (-ies)	Great Falls	Continental Divide
Judicial	Cattle		Granite Peak	Glacier National Park
Missouri River	Yellowstone National Park	Butte	Copper	Territory (-ies)
Executive Branch	Grizzly Bear(s)	Borders (-ed)	Oregon Treaty	Lewis and Clark

Montana Bingo

Fort Benton	Industry (-ies)	Reservation(s)	Great Falls	County (-ies)
Cattle	Oregon Treaty	Gold	Bison	Makoshika State Park
Crop(s)	Gemstone(s)		Great Plains	Climate
Grizzly Bear(s)	Yellowstone National Park	Copper	Butte	Blackspotted Cutthroat Trout
Executive Branch	Ponderosa Pine	Continental Divide	Maiasaura	Missouri River

Montana Bingo: Card No. 14

Montana Bingo

Lewis and Clark	Great Falls	Reservation(s)	Flag	Judicial
Blackspotted Cutthroat Trout	Great Plains	Billings	Bitterroot	County (-ies)
Sacajawea	Oregon Treaty		Union	Makoshika State Park
Executive Branch	Gold	Fort Peck Dam	Yellowstone National Park	Crop(s)
Maiasaura	Motto	Borders (-ed)	Flathead	Granite Peak

Montana Bingo

Butte	Gold	Fort Peck Dam	Flathead	Nickname
Ponderosa Pine	Continental Divide	Glacier National Park	Louisiana Purchase	Gemstone(s)
Crop(s)	Bluebunch Wheatgrass		Sacajawea	Granite Peak
Legislature	Cattle	Executive Branch	Lewis and Clark	Territory (-ies)
County (-ies)	Sioux	Borders (-ed)	Motto	Makoshika State Park

Montana Bingo

Climate	Rocky Mountains	Helena	Gold	Fort Benton
Lewis and Clark	County (-ies)	Yellowstone National Park	Gemstone(s)	Glacier National Park
Great Falls	Missouri River		Sioux	Fort Peck Dam
Grizzly Bear(s)	Maiasaura	Territory (-ies)	Reservation(s)	Continental Divide
Missoula	Crop(s)	Flag	Judicial	Bluebunch Wheatgrass

Montana Bingo

Flathead	Copper	Cattle	Crop(s)	Ponderosa Pine
Makoshika State Park	Climate	Missoula	Sacajawea	County (-ies)
Great Falls	Continental Divide		Helena	Bitterroot
Bluebunch Wheatgrass	Billings	Yellowstone National Park	Territory (-ies)	Great Plains
Sioux	Gold	Reservation(s)	Rocky Mountains	Blackspotted Cutthroat Trout

Montana Bingo

Sacajawea	Blackspotted Cutthroat Trout	Gold	Fort Peck Dam	Territory (-ies)
Lewis and Clark	Judicial	Makoshika State Park	Flag	Gemstone(s)
Rocky Mountains	Copper		Bison	Union
Great Plains	Sioux	Missoula	Motto	Helena
Bitterroot	Nickname	Maiasaura	Missouri River	Borders (-ed)

Montana Bingo: Card No. 19

Montana Bingo

Fort Benton	Rocky Mountains	Judicial	Gold	Borders (-ed)
Cattle	Granite Peak	Louisiana Purchase	Missoula	Ponderosa Pine
Bluebunch Wheatgrass	Glacier National Park		Legislature	Billings
River(s)	Western Meadowlark(s)	Seal	Motto	Sioux
Songs	Missouri River	Nickname	Territory (-ies)	Helena

Montana Bingo: Card No. 20

Montana Bingo

Lewis and Clark	Blackspotted Cutthroat Trout	Louisiana Purchase	Gold	River(s)
Bluebunch Wheatgrass	Helena	Butte	Fort Peck Dam	Oregon Treaty
Continental Divide	Maiasaura		Rocky Mountains	Reservation(s)
Missoula	Flag	Sioux	Grizzly Bear(s)	Missouri River
Legislature	Nickname	Borders (-ed)	Climate	Motto

Montana Bingo

Flathead	Great Plains	Helena	Bitterroot	Crop(s)
Ponderosa Pine	Judicial	Union	Fort Peck Dam	Bison
Cattle	Gemstone(s)		Oregon Treaty	Glacier National Park
Sioux	Grizzly Bear(s)	Motto	Billings	Louisiana Purchase
Nickname	Climate	Rocky Mountains	Continental Divide	Legislature

Montana Bingo: Card No. 22

Montana Bingo

Butte	Rocky Mountains	Flag	Bitterroot	Borders (-ed)
Blackspotted Cutthroat Trout	Fort Benton	Maiasaura	Lewis and Clark	Billings
Great Plains	Crop(s)		Seal	Oregon Treaty
Continental Divide	Nickname	Sioux	Climate	Motto
River(s)	Western Meadowlark(s)	Missouri River	Missoula	Helena

Montana Bingo

Butte	Missouri River	Fort Benton	Rocky Mountains	Fort Peck Dam
Helena	Borders (-ed)	Louisiana Purchase	Ponderosa Pine	Oregon Treaty
Glacier National Park	Flathead		Crop(s)	Continental Divide
River(s)	Seal	Sioux	Climate	Bluebunch Wheatgrass
Songs	Legislature	Nickname	Judicial	Western Meadowlark(s)

Montana Bingo: Card No. 24

Montana Bingo

Legislature	Louisiana Purchase	Rocky Mountains	Reservation(s)	Helena
Billings	Bluebunch Wheatgrass	Lewis and Clark	Butte	Bison
Grizzly Bear(s)	Fort Peck Dam		Seal	Sioux
Union	River(s)	Western Meadowlark(s)	Nickname	Gemstone(s)
Borders (-ed)	Fort Benton	Cattle	County (-ies)	Songs

Montana Bingo

Helena	Rocky Mountains	Great Plains	Ponderosa Pine	Flathead
Missoula	Judicial	Fort Peck Dam	Fort Benton	Butte
Grizzly Bear(s)	Seal		Gemstone(s)	Legislature
Climate	Bitterroot	River(s)	Nickname	Sioux
Glacier National Park	County (-ies)	Reservation(s)	Western Meadowlark(s)	Songs

Montana Bingo: Card No. 26

Montana Bingo

Great Plains	Cattle	Rocky Mountains	Fort Benton	Granite Peak
River(s)	Seal	Lewis and Clark	Sioux	Bison
Yellowstone National Park	Western Meadowlark(s)		Nickname	Legislature
Flathead	Blackspotted Cutthroat Trout	Louisiana Purchase	Songs	Billings
County (-ies)	Gemstone(s)	Helena	Union	Glacier National Park

Montana Bingo

Great Plains	Fort Benton	Union	Rocky Mountains	Butte
Granite Peak	Helena	Seal	Ponderosa Pine	Gemstone(s)
Western Meadowlark(s)	Continental Divide		Glacier National Park	Missoula
Territory (-ies)	Flathead	Maiasaura	Nickname	Sioux
Bitterroot	Great Falls	County (-ies)	Songs	River(s)

Montana Bingo: Card No. 28

Montana Bingo

Helena	Fort Benton	Flathead	Lewis and Clark	Great Falls
Motto	Missoula	Louisiana Purchase	Glacier National Park	Union
Grizzly Bear(s)	Seal		Bison	Rocky Mountains
Granite Peak	River(s)	Industry (-ies)	Nickname	Sioux
Butte	Fort Peck Dam	Songs	Blackspotted Cutthroat Trout	Western Meadowlark(s)

Montana Bingo: Card No. 29

Montana Bingo

Copper	Rocky Mountains	Ponderosa Pine	Great Falls	Sioux
Billings	Fort Benton	Great Plains	Gemstone(s)	Bison
Grizzly Bear(s)	Crop(s)		Glacier National Park	Louisiana Purchase
Songs	Blackspotted Cutthroat Trout	Bitterroot	Nickname	Seal
River(s)	Sacajawea	Western Meadowlark(s)	Helena	Union

Montana Bingo: Card No. 30